Planning Worship

Planning Worship

A Lay Servant Ministries Advanced Course

TAYLOR BURTON-EDWARDS

DISCIPLESHIP RESOURCES

PO BOX 340003 • NASHVILLE, TN 37203-0003
www.discipleshipresources.org

ISBNs
Print 978-0-88177-682-9
Mobi 978-0-88177-683-6
Epub 978-0-88177-684-3

At the time of publication all websites referenced in this book were valid. However, due to the fluid nature of the Internet some addresses may have changed, or the content may no longer be relevant.

The designation *UMH* refers to *The United Methodist Hymnal*. Copyright © 1989 The United Methodist Publishing House.

The designation *URWB* refers to the *Upper Room Worshipbook*. Copyright © 2006 Upper Room Books.

The designation *UMBW* refers to *The United Methodist Book of Worship*. Copyright © 1992 Abingdon.

The designation *WS* refers to *Worship and Song*. Copyright © 2011 Abingdon.

The designation *TFWS* refers to *The Faith We Sing*. Copyright © 2000 Abingdon.

Scripture quotations are from the New Revised Standard Version Bible © 1989, Division of Christian Education of the National Council of the Churches of Christ in the United States of America. Used by permission. All rights reserved.

Library of Congress Control Number:

Printed in the United States of America

DR 682

CONTENTS

THOUGHTS ON TEACHING
AND LEARNING

Each of us has a personal and unique learning style. It may be similar to that of others, but if we are able to use a learning style tailored to the way our brain recognizes, stores, and processes information, learning becomes easy and fun, and information is more effectively retained. Think of how you prefer to learn. Perhaps you are a reader. Maybe you learn more easily and efficiently by listening to music, to other sounds, or to voice. Perhaps you learn best in a "hands-on" manner. If the teaching method suits your learning style, you can process and adapt any information quickly. Addressing the educational needs of all students during a session may require you to modify your presentation style.

While lecture alone is the least effective means of presenting material, group activity is one of the most effective. Relational activities in small groups, or sometimes in the larger class context, associate students with different learning styles and thereby offer a way for the teacher to expose students to multiple avenues of learning. Although some sessions will lend themselves to one or more specific learning styles, the instructor can use a combination to address the needs of the students. As teachers, we need to be creative!

Articles and guidelines concerning multiple intelligences refer to the research of Howard Gardner, or the "eight ways of learning." These disciplines can be loosely grouped into three categories, or styles: auditory, visual, or tactile (also known as kinesthetic, as it can involve any form of participatory motion or perceived movement). Here are some activity suggestions:

Auditory
Class discussion
Show-and-tell
Creative rhythms and raps
Debate
Paraphrase or description
Music, songs, or rhymes
Poetry, storytelling, and reading
Word games
Seminars

Visual
Charts and graphs
Time lines and diagrams
Cartoons and bulletin boards
Photographs and videos
Posters
Journal writing
Montages, collages, and collections

Tactile
Games and simulations
Puppets
Sculpting
Drama, dance, and role-playing
Singing
Construction
Experiments
Origami and jigsaw puzzles

INTRODUCTION

TO THE COURSE LEADER

This advanced course is an elective for all Lay Servants. It builds on the course *Leading Worship* and presumes that participants have already taken it. This course is grounded in the principles and practices of planning worship. We want you and your class to know more *about* worship planning than when you began this course. Readings, classwork, and assignments between class sessions will help with this. But more important is that you and your class get into your bones and breath *how* to plan worship that is appropriate for the contexts in which you serve.

EXPECTATIONS

So you can devote class sessions as much to the *hows* as the *whats* of worship planning, you as well as participants should consistently:

1. Complete all the assigned readings before each class session, and bring from those readings a list of the three most important learnings and the three most significant questions the readings raised for you. Each session offers participants time to share and address these insights and questions.
2. Come ready to learn and strengthen key skills in planning worship. The daily Body Work skills practice assignments between sessions help you do this. Do these each day yourself, and encourage and support your class in doing them daily as well.
3. Come prepared to share with others, be vulnerable to others, and learn from others. Your role as leader is not to be the expert. Instead, you are there to coach others in

their learning, answer questions when you can, and point to resources participants can use to learn and grow.

4. Help everyone actively participate in learning and conversation. Lay Servants who are learning how to plan worship will have perspectives and experiences to contribute to the class as valuable as those who have been involved in planning worship for many years. Sometimes those with more experience or stronger personalities may try to dominate the conversation. Your role as leader is to make sure that each person in the class is given the opportunity to share in both small-group and plenary discussions.

DESIGN OF THE COURSE

This course includes ten hours of classroom time (five two-hour sessions), plus additional out-of-class assignments, including reading assignments and practice between sessions. It may be offered over a period of five weeks, three weeks, or even in an overnight retreat setting. A three-session model might use Session One for an introductory session, Sessions Two through Four for a weekend session, and Session Five for a closing session. An overnight retreat model might begin with Session One in the evening, Sessions Two through Four in the morning and on into the afternoon, and Session Five during the late afternoon and evening.

However you divide the content, begin each session with worship. You will find suggestions for opening worship grounded in the historic patterns of morning, midday, evening or night prayer as found in *The United Methodist Book of Worship* in the addendum. Choose the pattern that corresponds best to the time you hold your class sessions. Morning Prayer is appropriate at any time before noon. Midday prayer is appropriate from late morning to early afternoon. Evening Prayer, or vespers, is appropriate from late afternoon to early evening (just after sunset). Night prayer is held well after sundown. These forms of prayer give participants opportunities to take on a variety of different forms of leadership in your worshiping community (greeter, liturgist, reader, song leader, prayer leader). A consistent pattern of worship with a few weekly variations across the sessions will help deepen your sense of being "one with Christ, one with each other, and one in ministry to all the world."

Plan to be the primary worship leader for the first session, and invite the strongest leaders in the group to lead various elements of it with you (reading, praying/singing/chanting the Psalms, leading prayers, leading singing) as their skills and your skills best allow. Your first experiences in worship together will set the standard both for future worship experiences and for participants' expectations about how they may lead worship. For the first service, ask those who will lead with you to arrive twenty minutes early to rehearse the service, focusing on smooth transitions between parts.

BASIC RESOURCES

The basic texts for this course are *The Worship Workshop* by Marcia McFee and *The United Methodist Book of Worship*. Each participant will need a copy of these books. They can be ordered through Cokesbury.com or Amazon.com.

The Bible is our primary authority and primary worship resource. Each participant needs a Bible. It will help if participants bring the version used most frequently where they worship.

Be sure to have enough copies of *The United Methodist Hymnal*, *The Faith We Sing*, and *Worship and Song* for use during class sessions. There is a PowerPoint presentation available for the SLICE section of Session Five (http://www.gbod.org/slice-overview).

PREPARATION

Before the course begins, make sure all participants have a copy of the two required texts in order to prepare for the first session. Make sure the space in which you will meet is equipped with a chalkboard, dry-erase board, or sheets of newsprint/flipchart. Bring with you to each session a bowl of water, candle, and bell or chime.

Be sure the gathering space is conducive to both worship and learning. Consider using round tables rather than rows of chairs. This will help facilitate conversation and small-group activities. Make sure any audiovisual equipment you plan to use is in working order and that persons are available to operate it.

As the course leader, you should always be prepared. Pray and read scripture daily. Set aside time for silence. Fast if this is a helpful preparatory discipline for you. Ask others to pray with you and for you. Attend to God and be alert to the promptings of the Holy Spirit. Read the required texts and note three insights and three questions before each session that you will share with the class. Familiarize yourself with *The United Methodist Hymnal* (particularly the indexes), *The United Methodist Book of Worship*, *The Faith We Sing* and *Worship and Song* in order to draw from these resources and help class participants draw from them as well.

Create ways for participants to communicate with you and one another between class sessions. Consider creating a Facebook Group or Google+ circle for your class, and encourage interaction by posting class-related questions, insights, links, or helpful resources. This may also be a way for you to share and gain interaction around your three insights and three questions for each session's readings. You can also encourage class members to post their insights and questions for each session. You might create a Twitter account and plan a "TweetUp" once a week. At the very least, collect e-mail addresses and phone numbers of participants, and be sure to contact each class member between sessions. Creating channels of communication and interaction will help class members incorporate the content of the class into their own thoughts and practices, as well as enhance the sense of community and collaborative learning during and beyond class sessions.

Finally, remember that the first session will set the tone for the entire course. Prepare yourself well—body, mind, and spirit. Come to each session gracious and available—both to the Spirit and to participants. Commend yourself, the class, and your time together to the wisdom, grace, and love of the triune God.

ASSIGNMENT FOR THE FIRST SESSION

Read *The Worship Workshop: Creative Ways to Design Worship Together*, chapter 4, 60–77, and "An Energy Map for Worship," http://umcworship.blogspot.com/2013/02/an-energy-map-for-worship.html.

Planning Worship as a Team

OPENING WORSHIP (15 MINUTES)

Suggested forms for opening worship services can be found in the addendum. You will find additional resources in *The United Methodist Book of Worship*, 568–71 (morning), 572–73 (midday), 574–76 (evening), 577–79 (night), and 220–22 (music), and in the *Upper Room Worshipbook*, 8–30. Set the lighting and other elements you need for opening worship (candle, bowl of water, bell or chime). Place a bowl filled with water at the entrance of the classroom or worship space. As persons enter the space, greet them by saying, "Remember you are baptized, and be thankful." Using only gestures, invite persons to use the water as they wish. When all have entered and taken their seats, ring a bell or chime to signal the start of the opening worship.

LEARNING GOAL (5 MINUTES)

The goal for this session is to learn how to form an effective worship planning team and to form key practices for planning worship with vitality and integrity.

INSIGHTS AND QUESTIONS (20 MINUTES)

This is the opening work segment of each session. Invite participants to share three insights and three questions they have from the assigned readings. Capture these questions and insights on a chalkboard, dry-erase board, or flipchart that is visible to all participants.

BREAK (5 MINUTES)

KEY CONTENT (45 MINUTES)

INTRODUCTION

Use the following script as a guide to get started. You may wish to distribute copies of "Five Basic Principles of Worship" from *Worshiping with United Methodists: A Guide for Pastors and Church Leaders* by Hoyt Hickman.

There are three major approaches to worship planning: solo planning, "siloed" planning, and team-based planning. Solo worship planning means the pastor or another individual (perhaps a music director) plans most or all of each week's worship service alone. This is perhaps the easiest approach for the pastor or planner since it involves no consultation or coordination with the work of others. It also significantly limits the ability of worship to include the gifts and perspectives of *all* the people. This runs counter to both Principles 2 and 4 for worship Hoyt Hickman discusses in *Worshiping with United Methodists*: "Active congregational participation is crucial" and "worship should be relevant and inclusive" (18). Persons may not participate as easily in worship when they have no role in its planning. Worship planned by one individual is unlikely to be inclusive of the gifts and perspectives of the people as worship planned by a larger group.

The second approach to worship planning is "siloed" planning. In siloed planning, the work of worship planning is divided among a select group of "experts," each of whom plans parts of worship independently of one another. The most common example is a pastor who may select the scriptures and sermon topic and a music director who may select all of the music. While this may result in better participation by the congregation than solo planning, "siloed" worship planning may still feel disjointed and "cobbled together."

A third approach to planning worship is to develop a worship planning team or teams. The core members of a worship planning team are the pastor, the lead musician, an artist, someone who focuses on the design of the worship space, and representatives from technical teams (sound, computers, graphics, lighting, and so on) and helping teams (altar guild, Communion stewards, ushers, and greeters). A worship planning team functions best when at least one of its members is a "wise person" who knows the congregation well enough to understand how to stretch the capacity of the people and when to say, No. The ideal team brings a mix of ages, cultures, and, when possible, ethnicities to the table.

A worship planning team maximizes the congregation's capacity to live out all five principles of worship discussed in *Worshiping with United Methodists*. In the worship planning process, the team focuses on scripture (Principle 1). The varied social networks of the core team plus other teams you may invite to be involved for seasonal planning or planning for special occasions are likely to encompass your entire congregation as well as persons from the community (Principle 2). Worship planned by a varied group or groups is more likely to be spontaneous, diverse, and relevant, while continuing to maintain a consistent sense of order from season to season and from week to week (Principles 3 and 4). A rich collection of persons, social networks, and gifts is more likely to help the congregation feel "one with Christ, one with each other, and one in ministry to all the world" in the worship they plan together (Principle 5).

ASSEMBLE THE TEAMS

To facilitate learning and to practice this model, invite the class to form two worship planning teams (more if necessary, depending on the number of participants). Each team needs at least one musician (someone who has some degree of musical training and a sense of what songs to choose), a pastor/teacher/writer, an artist (who may also be a space designer), a tech person (sound, lighting, computer, video) and a wise person. Adapt the number of persons on each planning team and their roles based on the number of persons enrolled in the course. When the teams are assembled, allow time for team members to identify themselves and indicate which role they are assuming.

STUDY THE SCRIPTURES

Distribute this list of the Gospel readings for Advent, Year A to all team members: Matthew 24:36-44, Matthew 3:1-12, Matthew 11:2-11, and Matthew 1:18-25. Note that in a real worship planning team you would have considered all three readings and the Psalm for each Sunday, but for the sake of this exercise the class will focus only on the Gospel readings.

Invite the teams to spend the next few minutes reading the texts and noting of any images, music, ritual actions, themes, and questions that come to mind. You may wish to point the class to "Cross-Referencing Scripture," in *The Worship Workshop*, 70. Suggest that each person in the team choose one text, read it, and make notes on it. Try to cover all four texts. If the teams are larger than four persons each, more than one person may read and annotate each text.

BRAINSTORM ACROSS THE TEXTS

Before the brainstorming period, encourage the class to look at "IRIS" in *The Worship Workshop*, 66. Invite teams to assign a recorder and spend the next ten minutes sharing the images, music, ritual actions, or themes that come to mind for each text. Brainstorming is intended to be rapid, creative sharing "popcorn style," not a time for critique or further conversation. Anyone in the group may share any idea at any time.

IDENTIFY AN ANCHOR IMAGE AND THEMES

After all ideas are posted, have the recorder lead a conversation in which the team identifies an "anchor image," a theme for the season/series and subthemes related to the anchor image and theme for each service. Explain that an anchor image is an image or metaphor that lies behind and unites (anchors) all of the readings in the series you are considering. Marcia McFee describes it as "a visual metaphor that gives a series of services its symbolic focus." Ask each team to review all the images identified for each of the Sundays, noting in particular what images or metaphors recur or relate to all four. Have the teams choose the one image that seems to best unite them all. The anchor image will set the vision and tone for the feel and design of the entire series.

Invite the teams to work with the anchor image and the scriptures to build a theme statement for the series and a subtheme statement for each of the four weeks. Teams may wish to consult "Identifying a Theme," in *The Worship Workshop*, 69.

BUILD A ROUGH DRAFT OF A SERVICE

Now that each team has an anchor image, theme for the series, and subthemes for each week, have them use "The Basic Pattern of Worship" (*UMH*, 2 or *The Worship Workshop*, 73) to assemble the pieces already identified into a rough draft for a single service in the series. Ask the teams to use their brainstorming first, then add songs and liturgical elements from other resources (*Book of Worship, Worship and Song*) or ideas for new songs, prayers, or other ritual actions found or developed by team members in the coming weeks.

When teams have completed their rough drafts, display these on a wall for all to see. Encourage each team member to keep a copy of the rough draft and bring it to the next three sessions. During these sessions, teams will continue to refine their rough drafts and lead the class in worship based on the refined versions.

BREAK (5 MINUTES)

INSIGHTS FROM THIS SESSION (10 MINUTES)

Invite participants to work in pairs, preferably with someone from a different planning team. Ask the members of each pair to discuss one or two insights or an idea that has been reinforced for them during this session. After five minutes, invite the pairs to share one insight with the whole group. The group may discuss what each pair said if time allows.

QUESTIONS FROM THE READINGS (10 MINUTES)

Review the questions listed at the beginning of the session. Mark the questions that have already been answered during this session. Answer any remaining questions you can. Then decide and indicate how all unanswered questions will be addressed between now and the next session.

ASSIGNMENT (3 MINUTES)

BODY WORK: EMBODYING ENTRANCE AND PROCLAMATION/RESPONSE

This session's Body Work is about embodying the energy of the first two of the four movements of the Basic Pattern of Worship (addendum) and the transition between them as you have sketched these out in your rough draft.

The four movements are listed and described briefly in *The United Methodist Hymnal*, 2 (see addendum). They are described in more detail in *The United Methodist Book of Worship*,

16–32. The energy of each movement of worship is described in "An Energy Map for Worship" from this session's assigned readings.

After this session, participants should review the first two of the four movements of the Basic Pattern of worship and practice ways of embodying each movement and the transitions between movements to generate a smooth flow. For example, the energy of the Entrance is about getting bodies and minds in sync with praise to God in an energetic and kinetic way. How would you as the instructor position or move your body to represent this kind of energy (congregations often use processionals for this)? The energy of Word and Response begins with a more contemplative energy—listening to scripture read aloud and the sermon. How would you embody the energy of Word and Response (sitting? cupping your ear?)? How would you move smoothly between the more kinetic, energetic feel of the Entrance into the more contemplative, listening mode needed for Word and Response? You may find "An Energy Map for Worship" and the first three articles in the Bearings in Worship series helpful as you think through this in preparation for leading this session. You will find these listed in the reading assignments below.

Remind the class that persons are free to embody each of the elements and the transitions between them in his or her own way. Invite participants to do a quick run-through of this together, do it again at their homes near bedtime, and then again the following morning as part of their morning prayer time. As with the scripture reading exercise, class members should plan to do this each night and each morning until the next session.

ASSIGNMENT

Read *The Worship Workshop*, 19, 89–94, 106–7.

Read "Attentional Worship" http://umcworship.blogspot.com/2012/03/attentional-worship.html

Read "Bearings in Worship" http://umcworship.blogspot.com/2012/05/bearings-in-worship-series-map.html

Review "An Energy Map for Worship" http://umcworship.blogspot.com/2013/02/an-energy-map-for-worship.html

Note that "Attentional Worship" will be particularly valuable for this next class session as it includes several examples of successful transitions and bearings between the Entrance and

Proclamation/Response from diverse contexts and worship styles. The Bearings in Worship series will offer insight for the next three sessions.

For the blog entries listed in the readings, be sure to let class members know they are encouraged to post comments and questions.

Remind participants to bring their lists of three significant insights and three questions from the reading or Body Work to the next session or post them on the social media site you have created for the class.

Ask volunteers to lead the opening worship for the next session.

SENDING (2 MINUTES)

Choose a song from the services listed in the addendum appropriate for the time of day with which to close this session.

Leader: Go now in the peace and strength of Christ.
People: Thanks be to God.

Planning Entrance
and Proclamation/Response

OPENING WORSHIP (15 MINUTES)

Suggested forms for opening worship services can be found in the addendum. You will find additional resources in *The United Methodist Book of Worship*, 568–71 (morning), 572–73 (midday), 574–76 (evening), 577–79 (night), and 220–22 (music), and in the *Upper Room Worshipbook*, 8–30.

LEARNING GOAL (5 MINUTES)

The goal for this session is to practice and receive supportive feedback on planning the first two movements of the Basic Pattern of Worship.

INSIGHTS AND QUESTIONS (10 MINUTES)

Note the shorter period of time allotted for this section for both this session and the next. This allows more time for planning, leading, and feedback. You may wish to encourage class members to share more of their insights and questions via social media or e-mail between sessions.

KEY CONTENT: A WORSHIP WORKSHOP (60 MINUTES)

Below is a script you may use or adapt for the session.

INTRODUCTION

In the last session, you formed worship planning teams to experience an abbreviated form of a team worship planning process. In your teams, you identified an anchor image, an overarching theme for a series of services (Advent, Year A) and subthemes for each service in the series. You then brainstormed ideas for one of the services and assembled these, along with other resources, into a rough draft of that service. During this session and the next two, you will work in your teams to flesh out your rough draft, lead the class in worship with the service you develop, and receive feedback on your planning and leading. Your teams will also lead the class in a mini-service, focusing on one of the two major transitions between movements (Gathering to Entrance or Entrance to Word/Response).

INSTRUCTION: KEY POINTS IN WORSHIP PLANNING

Provide at least three copies of "Observations and Feedback for Worship Planners" (addendum) for each class participant. Teams that observe more than one service should be provided with additional copies. Persons who have taken *Leading Worship* may already be familiar with this form. The version for this class includes two additional elements, anchor image and space design. It also highlights local context more than the previous form. As you review the form with class participants, call particular attention to local context, space design, energy, flow, presence, and leadership.

LOCAL CONTEXT

All worship is local. It works because the people who are present can offer their gifts to God in ways that are authentic to their experience of God. The local context is far more than the location of the church building and the neighborhood around it. The local context is primarily composed of the stories and relationships (social networks) that the worshiping community uses to identify its life as a congregation. Keep this in mind as you refine your planning in this session and as you report on your local context to the larger group.

SPACE DESIGN

You may wish to make handouts (one per person or team) or project "What Affects Perceptions of Worship" as you discuss space design.

Participants may remember the handout from *Lay Servants Lead Worship*. That course focused primarily on energy, presence, leadership, and flow. It gave little attention to space and ambience. Worship leaders may have little direct control over these matters. But worship planners play a significant role in designing the worship space.

Careful worship planning gives attention to how the design of the space and the visual and multisensory elements in it may support or limit the ability of the worshiping community to offer itself fully to God in a worship service. Part of fleshing out your worship plans in the next three sessions is to pay attention to the ways you can use or arrange your worship space, elements already present within it, or elements you add (visuals, artwork, soundscapes, lighting) to help the space support the anchor image, series theme, and theme of the service.

ENERGY, FLOW, PRESENCE, AND LEADERSHIP

As you continue to refine your plans, receive feedback on those plans, lead the service and receive feedback on your leadership, give special attention to energy and flow. For energy, you may wish to review and refer to "An Energy Map for Worship." For flow, you may find "Bearings before the Entrance" and "Bearing Between Entrance and Word" most helpful.

For worship leaders, presence relates to embodying the "energy of the moment," and leadership is about keeping the flow of energy moving among the worshipers in each action and from one action/movement to the next. The presence and leadership of worship leaders is made easier and more effective when worship planners have planned the worship service with energy and flow (and therefore presence and leadership) in mind.

As you plan and review your sample service pieces for this session, do so with a sharp sense of how the planning and leading of the service embodies the energy needed and makes it possible for a smooth flow of energy to occur from one action to the next with minimum distractions or misdirections.

TEAM PLANNING

After your presentation, invite the teams to use the draft of the worship service they developed in the previous session and insights from readings, class instruction, and handouts to continue planning and refining each element of the first two movements of worship (Entrance and Proclamation/Response). Remind the class to pay attention to the items on the evaluation sheet, and to draw on the identified gifts and roles of each team member as they flesh out, prepare, and rehearse their service. The result of this planning period should be a fairly complete worship bulletin for the first two movements to distribute to all class participants, with some indication of the elements that will constitute the mini-service.

Teams are not expected to plan a full sermon (a title and a one-sentence description in the bulletin is sufficient). For the mini-service, pick one of the two bearings (either Gathering to Entrance, or Entrance to Word/Response) and plan to lead one or two elements before and after the bearings to show how you have designed a smooth transition in energy between these different movements in worship.

Plan Evaluation

At the end of the planning time, teams should pair up and share their worship bulletins and mini-services with one another. As they share their plans, they should also report the items listed at the top of the "Observations and Feedback for Worship Planners" handout. The evaluating team will provide its feedback using the handout and share observations about how well the proposed plan addresses energy and flow and both encouragement and suggestions for improvement.

Break

Regroup and Prepare for the Mini-Services

Based on feedback from the plan evaluation, team members should focus on strengthening and preparing the elements of their mini-service.

Mini-Services and Evaluation

Each team will meet with another team (if possible) and lead the combined group in their mini-service. Each team begins with a brief presentation to identify its members, the anchor image for the series, the theme for the series, the theme of the service, the design of the worship space, and some information about the local context of the service (from the "Observations and

Feedback for Worship Planners" handout). Members of the observing team should note these pieces of information on their evaluation forms.

After each team has led its mini-service, allow two minutes for the other team members to complete the evaluation forms, including observations about presence and leadership. Ask for volunteers to share their comments about leadership, space design, energy, transitions, and presence. Plan to allow half as much time for this feedback as the length of the service itself.

BREAK (5 MINUTES)

INSIGHTS FROM THIS SESSION (10 MINUTES)

Invite participants to work in pairs, preferably with someone from a different planning team. Ask the members of each pair to discuss one or two insights or an idea that has been reinforced for them during this session. After five minutes, invite the pairs to share one insight with the whole group. The class may discuss what each pair said if time allows.

QUESTIONS FROM THE READINGS (5 MINUTES)

Review the questions listed at the beginning of the session. Mark the questions that have already been answered during the session. Answer any remaining questions you can. Then decide and indicate how all unanswered questions will be addressed between now and the next session.

ASSIGNMENT (5 MINUTES)

BODY WORK: EMBODYING THE SECOND AND THIRD MOVEMENTS OF THE BASIC PATTERN OF WORSHIP AND THE TRANSITION/BEARINGS BETWEEN THEM

The Body Work this week focuses on embodying the second and third movements of the Basic Pattern of Worship and the transition/bearings between them. Instruct the class that the energy at the end of Proclamation/Response moves from congregational prayer toward the multisensory act of congregational praise (the Great Thanksgiving), which includes the kinetic acts of moving, receiving, eating, and reflecting.

Remind the class that persons are free to embody each of the elements and the transitions in his or her own way. Invite participants to do a quick run-through of this together, do it again at their homes near bedtime, and then again the following morning as part of their morning prayer time. As with the scripture reading exercise, class members should plan to do this each night and each morning until the next session.

Read *The Worship Workshop*, 40–45, 100, 102–104.

Review "Attentional Worship"

   http://umcworship.blogspot.com/2012/03/attentional-worship.html

Review "Bearings in Worship"

   http://umcworship.blogspot.com/2012/05/bearings-in-worship-series-map.html

Review "Between Word/Response and Table"

   http://umcworship.blogspot.com/2011/04/bearings-part-iii-d-between.html

Review "An Energy Map for Worship"

   http://umcworship.blogspot.com/2013/02/an-energy-map-for-worship.html

Remind participants to bring their lists of three significant insights and three questions from the reading or Body Work to the next session or post them on the social media site you have created for the class.

Ask volunteers to lead the opening worship for the next session.

SENDING (5 MINUTES)

Choose a song from the services listed in the addendum appropriate for the time of day with which to close this session.

Leader: Go now in the peace and strength of Christ.

People: Thanks be to God.

Planning Word/Response
through Thanksgiving/Communion

OPENING WORSHIP (10 MINUTES)

Suggested forms for opening worship services can be found in the addendum. You will find additional resources in *The United Methodist Book of Worship*, 568–71 (morning), 572–73 (midday), 574–76 (evening), 577–79 (night), and 220–22 (music), and in the *Upper Room Worshipbook*, 8–30.

LEARNING GOAL (5 MINUTES)

The goal for this session is to practice and get supportive feedback on planning the second and third movements of the Basic Pattern of Worship and the transition between them.

INSIGHTS AND QUESTIONS (10 MINUTES)

Note the shorter period of time allotted for this section for both this session and the next. This allows more time for planning, leading, and feedback. You may wish to encourage class members to share more of their insights and questions via social media or e-mail between sessions.

KEY CONTENT: A WORSHIP WORKSHOP (60 MINUTES)

Provide participants at least three copies of the "Observation and Feedback for Worship Planners" handout found in the addendum. Teams will use one copy to develop their own services. The second copy should be used to provide evaluative feedback on the plans presented by other teams. The third copy is to provide evaluative feedback on both plans and leadership of the mini-service participants will lead later in the session. Below is a script you may use or adapt for the session.

INTRODUCTION

In the previous session, you refined your plans for the first two movements of worship, received feedback on those plans, led a mini-service with elements before and after a significant transition, and received feedback on your revisions and leadership. During this session you will develop, refine, lead, and receive feedback on the transition from the second and the third movements of worship—Word/Response and Holy Communion.

INSTRUCTION: THE MOST CHALLENGING TRANSITION

The transition between Word/Response and Table can be among the most challenging to plan and lead smoothly (see the Bearings in Worship series). United Methodists, along with other Protestants, are still in the early stages of understanding Sunday worship in terms of both Word *and* Table in an integrated way. Our teaching document on Holy Communion, *This Holy Mystery: A United Methodist Understanding of Holy Communion* passed by General Conference in 2004 and reaffirmed in 2012, marked the first time any Methodist body with a substantial base in the United States clearly stated, "The complete pattern of Christian worship for the Lord's Day is Word and Table—the gospel is proclaimed in both Word and sacrament." The document calls all United Methodists to move toward celebration of Holy Communion at least once a week, 18–19.

Many United Methodist congregations in the United States have followed suit. In 1992, Hoyt Hickman, who was at that time Director of Worship Resources at the General Board of Discipleship, led a research project to discover the number of United Methodist congregations celebrating weekly Communion as a principle service of worship. He found a total of seventeen congregations. The 2004–2007 Music and Worship Study found that 7 percent of United

Methodist congregations celebrate Communion weekly. If the sample chosen for this study is representative of the whole, it would suggest that at least two thousand five hundred congregations celebrate Communion each week.

As more congregations are celebrating Holy Communion on a weekly basis, many congregations are discovering new and effective ways to order their services (see *The United Methodist Hymnal* and *The United Methodist Book of Worship*). Your role as worship planner is critical not only to enabling the smooth transition between the movements of Word/Response and Thanksgiving/Communion but also in helping United Methodists reclaim the centrality of Word *and* Sacrament to worship.

As you refine your planning for the final elements of Word/Response and the celebration of Holy Communion during this session, do so with particular attention to connecting the Response to the Word (based on your anchor image and theme for this service) and the celebration around the Lord's table that follows.

Team Planning

Invite teams to use the draft of the outline for worship they developed in the first session and the bulletin for the first two movements developed in the previous session, along with insights from the readings and class instruction, to refine their plans for the Response to the Word and the celebration of Holy Communion. Remind participants of the importance of the Invitation to the Table, Confession of Sin, Pardon, Peace, and Offering, as well as the Great Thanksgiving. Teams may write their own Confession of Sin and Pardon. They are not expected to develop a Great Thanksgiving for this service.

In addition to the more complete service bulletin, participants will develop for these two movements, teams should also identify their mini-service—the one or two elements that culminate the Word/Response movement and the first two or three elements that begin the Thanksgiving/Communion movement. Teams will lead this mini-service and receive feedback both on their planning and their leadership later in the session.

Plan Evaluation

At the end of the planning time, teams should pair up and share their worship bulletins and mini-services with one another. As they share their plan, they should also report the items listed at the top of the "Observations and Feedback for Worship Planners" handout. The evaluating team will provide its feedback using the handout and share observations about how well the proposed plan addresses energy and flow and offer encouragement and suggestions for improvement.

BREAK

REGROUP AND PREPARE FOR THE MINI-SERVICES

Based on feedback from the plan evaluation, team members should focus on strengthening and preparing the elements of their mini-service.

MINI-SERVICES AND EVALUATION

Each team should meet with another team (if possible) and lead the combined group in their mini-service. Each team begins with a brief presentation to identify its members, the anchor image for the series, the theme for the series, the theme of the service, the design of the worship space, and information about the local context of the service (from the "Observations and Feedback for Worship Planners" handout). Members of the observing team may note these pieces of information on their evaluation forms.

After each team has led its mini-service, allow two minutes for the other team members to complete the evaluation forms, including observations about presence and leadership. Ask volunteers to share their comments about leadership, space design, energy, transitions, and presence. Plan to allow half as much time for this feedback as the length of the service itself.

BREAK (5 MINUTES)

INSIGHTS FROM THIS SESSION (10 MINUTES)

Invite participants to work in pairs, preferably with someone from a different planning team. Ask the members of each pair to discuss one or two insights or an idea that has been reinforced for them during this session. After five minutes, invite the pairs to share one insight with the whole group. The class may discuss what each pair said if time allows.

QUESTIONS FROM THE READINGS (10 MINUTES)

Review the questions listed at the beginning of the session. Mark the questions that have already been answered during the session. Answer any remaining questions you can. Then decide and indicate how all unanswered questions will be addressed between now and the next session.

ASSIGNMENT (5 MINUTES)

BODY WORK: FROM SUSTAINED GRATITUDE TO PARTING WITH A PURPOSE

The Body Work exercise between this session and the next focuses on helping participants get in touch with the transition in energy from the moments after receiving Holy Communion through the Sending.

Invite participants to stand. Say to the class, "With your bodies, show me 'sustained gratitude.'" Allow time for class members to move into their poses or gestures. Ask volunteers to share how their pose or gesture expresses sustained gratitude. After two or three responses say to the class, "Now, show me 'parting with a purpose'!" Allow time for participants to embody their poses or gestures, then invite two or three persons to share how they are embodying "parting with a purpose."

Ask participants to work out the transition or movement in their bodies and energy between the two poses they have just taken so that they are fully present in each. Ask one or two volunteers to share what they are doing and why it works for them.

Remind the class to practice this between now and the next session. Encourage them to practice this exercise while focusing on sustained gratitude, purposeful parting, and the transition between poses and gestures. Say to the class, "If you can in your bodies feel the transition between movements, you can better plan for all the bodies who gather in worship.

Read *The Worship Workbook*, 15–18, 98–9.
  Review "An Energy Map for Worship"
    http://umcworship.blogspot.com/2013/02/an-energy-map-for-worship.html

Review "Bearings in Worship: Between Table and Sending"
http://umcworship.blogspot.com/2011/04/bearings-part-iii-e-between-table-and.html
Remind participants to bring their lists of three significant insights and three questions from the reading or Body Work to the next session or post them on the social media site you have created for the class.

Ask volunteers to lead the opening worship for the next session

SENDING (5 MINUTES)

Choose a song from the services listed in the addendum appropriate for the time of day with which to close this session.

Leader: Go now in the peace and strength of Christ.
People: Thanks be to God.

Planning Thanksgiving/ Communion through Sending

OPENING WORSHIP (10 MINUTES)

Suggested forms for opening worship services can be found in the addendum. You will find additional resources in *The United Methodist Book of Worship* 568–71 (morning), 572–73 (midday), 574–76 (evening), 577–79 (night), and 220–22 (music), and in the *Upper Room Worshipbook*, 8–30.

LEARNING GOAL (5 MINUTE)

The goal for this session is to practice and receive supportive feedback on planning the last two movements of the Basic Pattern of Worship and the transition between them.

INSIGHTS AND QUESTIONS (10 MINUTES)

Note the shorter period of time allotted for this section for both this session and the next. This allows more time for planning, leading, and feedback. You may wish to encourage class members to share more of their insights and questions via social media or e-mail between sessions.

KEY CONTENT: A WORSHIP WORKSHOP (60 MINUTES)

Provide participants at least three copies of the "Observations and Feedback for Worship Planners" handout provided in the addendum. Teams will use one copy to develop their own services. The second copy should be used to provide evaluative feedback on the plans presented by other teams. The third copy is to provide evaluative feedback on both plans and leadership of the mini-service participants will lead later in the session. Below is a script you may use or adapt for your class.

Introduction

By now participants should know the routine for these workshops—planning, evaluation of planning, break, leading a mini-service, and evaluation of the mini-service. Remind the class of the planning for this week: the actions after Communion are received through the Sending.

Instruction: The Second Most Challenging Transition

The reading from the Bearings in Worship series highlighted for this session—the transition between Holy Communion and the Sending—can be the second most challenging aspect of worship to plan and lead smoothly. As discussed in the previous session, experience and certain historical factors continue to make this transition difficult for many worship planners and leaders.

Below are three historical patterns that may inhibit the planning and leading of a smooth transition or accomplishing what each of these two movements is designed to accomplish.

(1) The practice of Holy Communion and the actions that follow it are often understood as primarily individual and often penitential experiences. The congregation may have participated actively and energetically in the Great Thanksgiving. Many people may be moving en masse, toward stations to receive the Body and Blood of Christ which they have just prayed will help them (plural) function as "the body [collective] of Christ redeemed by his blood" (*UMH*, 10). Still, the fact that we actually receive Communion *individually* can quickly turn this act of corporate worship into an act of individual devotion. We may shift rapidly and dramatically in our understanding of what is happening here from "the people of God in the company of God and one another" into "just me and Jesus."

A shift from corporate worship to personal worship and from public worship to private devotion during Communion may not be entirely bad. Jesus calls each of us by name. He comes to dwell in each of us individually; indeed, the Spirit moves in each of our hearts in profound

34

and distinct ways in the sacrament of Holy Communion. But our individual experiences, however meaningful they may be, are not the penultimate outcome. Rather, our individual experiences are meant to *flow back* and *flow out* into our corporate reality as "the body of Christ, redeemed by his blood" (*UMH*, 10). How we plan what happens after persons receive Holy Communion has much to do with how well the congregation can make a gracious transition from the "sustained corporate gratitude" of Communion to the "parting with a purpose" of the Sending.

Allow room for personal devotional acts and acts of corporate worship to occur simultaneously during Holy Communion. Attend to both. Trust the congregation to make its own transitions from public to personal to public again on its own—and the Spirit's—timetable. Some persons will need quiet, alone time with Jesus after receiving the elements. Others will be ready to sing a hymn. Attentive worship planners will create the space for personal worship *and* corporate worship that embodies sustained gratitude.

(2) A long history supports the belief that worship ends *rather than* sends. This week's Bearings in Worship article explored this idea in some depth. What we need to ask as worship planners is how will we help persons move beyond what may be an ingrained idea that the conclusion of worship is a quiet, dignified recession instead of a procession into the world in the name of Christ and in the power of the Holy Spirit?

First suggestion: Banish the word *recessional* from your church's vocabulary, your worship guides, your church newsletters, and any description you will ever publish from here forward about what is happening at the conclusion of your worship. Stop using the word cold turkey, and encourage others to do the same. Also banish the word *postlude* from the description of the music that accompanies worshipers on their procession into the world.

Second suggestion: Use the word *processional* or a similar word to describe everything that happens during this part of the service—processional hymn, processional anthem, processional music. You may not yet have the influence to make this vocabulary change in your congregation, but for this class, by all means, do so! And then do what you can to help spread the processional virus.

If you cannot change your congregation's language immediately, you can plan for actions that embody the propulsive energy of sending forth into the world in Christ's name and the Spirit's power. Include an indication to stand during this part of the service. Choose music with a strong beat that the congregation either knows or would be willing to sing at full voice. Choose words and phrases for prayers that are brief and exclamatory, phrases like "Go, team, go!" instead of "May you feel warm and peaceful as we part, until we meet again." Align these words and phrases in ways that build the energy progressively through the final acts of worship, rather than allowing a letdown at the end.

(3) A long history supports the belief that Holy Communion functions as an "add-on" to "regular" worship and the disruptive double ending. While our ritual offers us effective "bearings" between Holy Communion and Sending in the form of the Prayer of Thanksgiving after Communion, this prayer is also a relative newcomer to United Methodist worship practices, and, perhaps for the sake of time, is simply not used. This leaves no action that resynchronizes and refocuses the worshipers from what may be a wide variety of devotional acts toward the unified action of corporate worship that is intended in the Sending. Moving directly from what is often quiet devotion into a big send-off is not only jarring (think about this as shifting a manual transmission car in motion without engaging the clutch!) but also disruptive. The jarring and disruption is likely to be so prominent in the awareness of worshipers that the purpose of the Sending may not be fully realized. The service then lurches to its conclusion, with a double ending—the first abrupt, the second unsatisfying.

As you plan the acts that will move worshipers from "sustained gratitude" to "parting with a purpose" in this session, remember how you have practiced and perfected that transition in your body and awareness exercises since the last session. Use the wisdom your body has developed to guide you and your team toward the most effective expression of "sustained gratitude" and "parting with a purpose" and the transition between the two.

Team Planning

Invite the worship planning teams to use the draft of the outline for worship they developed two sessions ago and the more complete bulletin for the first two movements they developed during the previous session along with insights from the readings and class instruction to refine their plans for the Response to the Word and the celebration of Holy Communion. Remind participants of the importance of Invitation to the Table, Confession of Sin, Pardon, Peace, and Offering, as well as the Great Thanksgiving itself. Teams may write their own Confession of Sin and Pardon. They are not expected to develop a Great Thanksgiving for this service.

In addition to the more complete service bulletin participants should develop for these two movements, teams should also identify their mini-service, the one or two elements that culminate the Word/Response movement, and the first two or three elements that begin the

Thanksgiving/Communion movement. Teams will lead this mini-service and receive feedback both on their planning and their leadership later in the session.

PLAN EVALUATION

At the end of the planning time, teams should pair up and share their worship bulletins and mini-services with one another. As they share their plans, they should also report the items listed at the top of the "Observations and Feedback for Worship Planners" handout. The evaluating team provides its feedback using the handout and share observations about how well the proposed plan addresses energy and flow, offering encouragement and suggestions for improvement.

BREAK

REGROUP AND PREPARE FOR THE MINI-SERVICES

Based on feedback from the plan evaluation, team members will focus on strengthening and preparing the elements of the mini-service they will lead.

MINI-SERVICES AND EVALUATION

Each team should meet with another team (if possible) and lead the combined group in their mini-service. Each team begins with a brief presentation to identify its members, the anchor image for the series, the theme for the series, the theme of the service, the design of the worship space, and information about the local context of the service is (from the "Observations and Feedback for Worship Planners" handout). Members of the observing team may note these pieces of information on their evaluation forms.

After each team has led its mini-service, allow two minutes for the other team members to complete the evaluation forms, including observations about presence and leadership. Ask for volunteers to share their comments about leadership, space design, energy, transitions, and presence. Plan to allow half as much time for this feedback as the length of the service itself.

BREAK (5 MINUTES)

INSIGHTS FROM THIS SESSION (10 MINUTES)

Invite participants to work in pairs, preferably with someone from a different planning team. Ask the members of each pair to discuss one or two insights or an idea that has been reinforced for them during this session. After five minutes, invite the pairs to share one insight with the whole group. The class may discuss what each of the pairs said if time allows.

QUESTIONS FROM THE READINGS (10 MINUTES)

Review the questions listed at the beginning of the session. Mark the questions that have already been answered during this session. Answer any remaining questions you can. Then decide and indicate how all unanswered questions will be addressed between now and the next session.

ASSIGNMENT (5 MINUTES)

BODY WORK: PUTTING IT ALL TOGETHER

In the past three sessions, participants have been asked to embody the energy of the various movements of worship and the transitions between them. As they prepare for the final session they will work on embodying all four movements and the transitions between them, starting with the transition from the scattered energy of worshipers entering the worship space, the focused, synchronizing energy of the Entrance, the sustained, active, listening energy of Word/Response, the sustained joyful gratitude of Holy Communion, and the propulsive "parting with a purpose" of the Sending.

Participants are not expected to put everything together in this session, but as leader you should be prepared to give an example of how they might do so. Encourage the class to get started after this session and to continue their work on embodying all four movements and the transitions between them from now until the next session each evening before bed and each morning upon rising.

Ask volunteers to lead the opening worship for the next session.

ASSIGNMENT

Read and complete the exercises in *The Worship Workbook*, 21–31 and 46–59.

Read and answer the questions at the end of each section of "Planning Vital Weekly Worship,"
  http://www.gbod.org/content/uploads/legacy/kintera-files/WorshipPlanning3.pdf

Read "The Dynamics and Passions of Passionate Worship," http://www.gbod.org/content/
uploads/legacy/kintera/entry_7736/19/passion-tbemay2011.pdf

Participants should obtain and bring with them to the next session sample worship bulletins from at least three different services in the past year: a regular Sunday service, a special service (such as Christmas Eve), a service that includes a baptism, and a service that includes Communion (in addition to the Christmas Eve or other special service). They should also bring their completed service bulletin based on the work they have done in class during the past three sessions.

Remind participants to bring their lists of three significant insights and three questions from the reading or Body Work to the next session or post them on the social media site you have created for the class.

SENDING (5 MINUTES)

Choose a song from the services listed in the addendum appropriate for the time of day with which to close this session.

Leader: Go now in the peace and strength of Christ.
People: Thanks be to God.

Evaluating and Strengthening Vital United Methodist Worship (SLICE)

OPENING WORSHIP (15 MINUTES)

Suggested forms for opening worship services can be found in the addendum. You will find additional resources in *The United Methodist Book of Worship*, 568–71 (morning), 572–73 (midday), 574–76 (evening), 577–79 (night), and 220–22 (music), and in the *Upper Room Worshipbook*, 8–30.

LEARNING GOAL (5 MINUTES)

The goal for this session is to evaluate worship and worship planning for the service participants have designed for their own worship settings using the SLICE tool and worksheets along with other readings and resources from the course.

INSIGHTS AND QUESTIONS (25 MINUTES)

Invite the class to share at least one and as many as three questions or insights from the readings and Body Work assigned for this session. Use the remaining time to invite three to five volunteers to share the routine they developed since the last session to embody the energy of an entire worship service. Ask the volunteers to explain their routine and answer any questions from the class.

KEY CONTENT: EVALUATING WORSHIP (60 MINUTES)

Make several copies of each of the SLICE handouts in the addendum (pages 65–78) and place these on the tables before participants arrive. Each table should have several copies of "SLICE: CORE VALUES OF VITAL WORSHIP." Distribute copies of the other handouts to different tables. One table may have several copies of "Sacramental" and another have several copies of "Embodied," and so on. Remember that you may use the PowerPoint presentation mentioned on page 11 of this resource. Below is a script you may use or adapt for your class.

INTRODUCTION

With the readings and worksheets to prepare you for this session, you have been given a number of different ways to reflect on how worship is planned and led in your local congregation. As we have noted before, leadership in worship is critical to worship vitality, and effective planning of worship can go a long way to ensure that leaders have a strong foundation from which to help their congregation worship well.

Effective evaluation of the planning and leadership of worship is key to ongoing planning. Many congregations spend much energy on planning worship and little time evaluating how well or even *if* worship in their setting is the most vital expression of what United Methodist worship can be.

Two tendencies among worship leaders can prove divisive and counter-productive to evaluating worship:

> (1) Some congregations release surveys to learn the likes and dislikes of congregants or their worship preferences. Such surveys treat worshipers as consumers seeking their own satisfaction rather than the baptized who have gathered to

offer themselves to God in spirit and in truth. In a way, surveys promote idolatry and may also sustain, if not cause, worship wars within congregations.

(2) Some congregations approach worship evaluation primarily as a means to fix worship, and focus primarily on what is wrong with it or missing from it. Aspects of worship that are broken and obvious to all should be addressed. But simply fixing what is broken may be a drain on worship vitality rather than an enhancement to it. Worse yet, relying primarily on a fundamentally negative approach to evaluating worship ignores the abundant gifts of God's people and tends to generate a spirit of fear, judgment, and suspicion rather than joy, peace, and love in the Holy Spirit.

The SLICE tool provides a framework for evaluating worship in your setting and will help you identify what is *working well* in your worship and to *strengthen* your worship planning and leadership by *building on and deepening these strengths*. Instead of focusing on personal preferences, it helps worship planners, worship leaders, and the entire congregation focus on the ***core values*** of worship in our Wesleyan and larger Christian heritage. Thus, this tool that can help you evaluate and strengthen worship where you are regardless of your worship's style or genre.

Refer here to the first SLICE handout. Project it on a screen (PowerPoint) or write the acronym on five seperate sheets of adhesive flipchart paper and post them around the room.

Ideally, all United Methodist congregations would be strong in all five slices.

"S"— **Sacramental:** Congregations continue to grow in the richness of their sacramental life in worship and ministry.

"L"— **Liturgical:** Worship is primarily the work of the people, not simply the work of the "folks up front" or the production of the worship planning team.

"I"— **Indigenous:** Worship consistently reflects the best gifts of your particular people gathered in your particular time and place.

"C"— **Connected:** Worship is connected and continues to connect worshipers to Christ, to one another, to all Christians in all times and places, and to ministry that reaches all the world.

"E"— **Embodied:** Worship calls and enables worshipers to offer themselves to God in many ways, including with their bodies.

Remember that strengths and continual growth in all five of these categories is the *ideal*. It is also *achievable*. We can move toward this ideal by ***starting where we are*** and ***building on the strengths we already have***. Gratitude to God and one another for our strengths gives us the positive energy to grow and a solid foundation on which to build. Building from our strengths has the positive spillover effect of opening up new areas of strength we may not have had or recognized before. This is how we are led by the Holy Spirit "from strength to strength" (Ps. 84:7).

Based on the assigned readings for this session and the work you have done so far in the class, take a few minutes to think about the two SLICEs in which your congregation has the greatest strengths. (Allow participants a few minutes to reflect; continue when everyone is ready.)

Your work in the final session of this course is to ***discover*** ways worship and worship planning in your congregation may increase in vitality in these two SLICEs, to ***commit*** to one action you will take in each of these two areas in your congregation within the next six weeks to help increase vitality, and to ***select an accountability partner from the class*** as you complete the action you have committed to take and begin to discern next steps.

FIRST SLICE

Identify which SLICE questionnaires are on each table. Invite persons to move to a table with the first of the two areas of strengths they identified. Using the bulletins participants brought with them to class, plus information from the readings throughout the course, invite the class to complete the questionnaires and discuss their responses with others at the table. After discussing their responses, participants should then decide one action they can take to strengthen worship in this SLICE of their congregation, and select an accountability partner to encourage, support, and challenge them to complete the commitment and take a next step over the following six weeks. Groups may conclude their time by praying to be faithful to God, their congregation, and one another in the commitments they have made.

BREAK

SECOND SLICE

Follow the same steps for the second SLICE exercise as the first SLICE, only this time at a table with handouts focusing on the second "strong SLICE" participants have selected.

INSIGHTS FROM THIS SESSION AND THE COURSE (15 MINUTES)

Have participants work in pairs, preferably with a person whom they have not previously worked during the SLICE conversations. Ask each pair to discuss which two SLICE areas they chose and why, what they learned in the process, what they have committed to do to strengthen worship in those areas within their congregations, and at least one major lesson they have learned from this course. After approximately ten minutes, invite the pairs to share one of these commitments or learnings with the whole group, record the responses so they are visible to everyone in the class, and allow time for celebration of these commitments and learnings.

QUESTIONS FROM THE COURSE (15 MINUTES)

Review the questions listed at the beginning of the session. Mark the questions that have already been answered during the session. Answer any remaining questions you can. Open the floor to new questions that have arisen and remain unanswered from this session and any other session in the course. Allow time for discussion.

SENDING (5 MINUTES)

Choose a song from the services listed in the addendum appropriate for the time of day with which to close this session.

Leader: Go now in the peace and strength of Christ.
People: Thanks be to God.

Addendum

LETTER TO THE COURSE PARTICIPANT

This advanced course in Lay Servant Ministries is an elective for all Lay Servants. It builds on the course *Leading Worship* and presumes that participants have already taken it. This course is grounded in the principles and practices of planning worship. We want you to know more *about* worship planning than when you began this course. Readings and work in class and between class sessions will help with that. But more important is that you learn *how* to plan worship that is appropriate for the contexts in which you serve.

EXPECTATIONS

So that your class sessions can be devoted at least as much to the *hows* as the *whats* of worship planning, you should consistently:

1. Complete all the assigned readings before each class session, and glean from those readings a list of the three most important learnings and the three most significant questions the readings raised for you. Each session is designed to offer the class time to share and address these insights and questions.
2. Come ready to learn and strengthen key *skills* in planning worship. The daily Body Work assignments between sessions are there to help you do this. Do these each day.
3. Come prepared to share with others, be vulnerable to others, and learn from others.

BASIC RESOURCES

The basic texts for this course are *The Worship Workshop* by Marcia McFee, and *The United Methodist Book of Worship*. Each participant will need a copy of each book. These titles can be ordered through Cokesbury.com or Amazon.com.

The Bible is our primary authority and our primary worship resource. Each participant needs a Bible. It is helpful if each person brings the version used most frequently where he or she worships regularly.

ASSIGNMENT FOR THE FIRST SESSION

Read *The Worship Workshop: Creative Ways to Design Worship Together*, chapter 4, 60–77, and "An Energy Map for Worship," http://umcworship.blogspot.com/2013/02/an-energy-map-for-worship.html.

WORSHIP RESOURCES

MORNING PRAYER

Place a bowl of water (the baptismal bowl) at the entrance of the worship/class space. As persons enter the greeter says to them, "Name, remember you are baptized, and be thankful." A bell sounds, inviting silence. A candle is lit, and the liturgist interrupts the silence with the call to worship.

Liturgist: O Lord, open our lips.
All: And our mouths shall declare your praise.

Morning Song: If your class is small or wishes to worship in a contemplative style, choose from "O Splendor of God's Glory Bright" (*UMH*, no. 679), "Father, We Praise Thee" (*UMH*, no. 680), "Lord of All Hopefulness" (*URWB*, no. 179), or "Jesus in the Morning" (*URWB*, no. 183). If your class is large or wishes to worship in a more energetic style, consider "See the Morning Sun Ascending" (*UMH*, no. 674), "When Morning Gilds the Skies" (*URWB*, no. 184), "This Day God Gives Me" (*URWB*, no. 185), or "Gracious Creator of Sea and of Land" (*WS*, no. 3161). If you are really ambitious and have a solid keyboard accompanist or jazz combo, try "Sing of the Lord's Goodness" (*WS*, no. 3010).

Scripture

Session One: Isaiah 2:1-4
Session Two: Isaiah 11:1-10
Session Three: Isaiah 35:1-10

Session Four: Isaiah 7:10-16
Session Five: 1 Samuel 2:1-10

Silence (2 minutes)

Song (standing)

Session One: Canticle of Zechariah (*UMH*, no. 208)
Session Two: Canticle of Praise to God (*UMH*, no. 91)
Session Three: Canticle of God's Glory (*UMH*, no. 82 or 83)
Session Four: Canticle of the Holy Trinity (*UMH*, no. 80)
Session Five: Canticle of Thanksgiving (*UMH*, no. 74)

Prayer (standing)

Prayers of the People (Spoken: *UMH*, no. 877; Sung: *TFWS*, no. 2201, *WS*, no. 3125; additional prayer responses *WS*, no. 3133 and 3155)

Lead the prayer intercessions yourself, or invite another person to lead them. If you choose an arrangement to be sung, remember that singing for prayer is in a "normal" register, not an operatic or solo style. People may remain silent except for the responses, or they may lift up names of persons or situations related to each petition.

Conclude the intercessions with, "for the forgiveness of our sins."

Silence (1 minute)

Leader: Hear the good news. If we confess our sins, God is faithful and just and will forgive us our sins and cleanse us from all unrighteousness. In the name of Jesus Christ, we are forgiven.
People: **In the name of Jesus Christ, we are all forgiven.**
All: **Glory to God, *Amen*.**

Lord's Prayer

Blessing

Leader: Let us go forth rejoicing in the strength of the Holy Spirit.
People: **Thanks be to God.**

The peace

MIDDAY PRAYER

This service may begin with the ringing of a bell and a brief period of silence as all rise to their feet.

Scripture

Isaiah 40:30-31

Prayer of Thanksgiving (*UMBW, no. 572*)

Song

In addition to the hymns suggested in *The United Methodist Book of Worship*, no. 572, you might also wish to consider the following: "We Will Glorify the King of Kings" (*TFWS*, no. 2087), "Come and See" (*TFWS*, no. 2127), "Come and Find the Quiet Center" (*TFWS*, no. 2128), "Blessed Quietness" (*TFWS*, no. 2142), "I'm So Glad Jesus Lifted Me" (*TFWS*, no. 2151), "I'm Gonna Live So God Can Use Me" (*TFWS*, no. 2153), "Shine, Jesus, Shine" (*TFWS*, no. 2173), "Breath of God, Breath of Peace" (*WS*, no. 3145), "Welcome" (*WS*, no. 3152), "The Lord of Life a Vine Is He" (*WS*, no. 3155).

At this interval persons may be invited to pray aloud as the Spirit leads.

The Lord's Prayer

Blessing

Leader: Jesus Christ is with us.
People: The Holy Spirit is in this place.
Leader: Go in God's peace, sharing peace.

The Peace

EVENING PRAYER

Begin with silence (about one minute) after ringing the bell or chime. Continue in silence as you light a candle. Interrupt the silence with the opening of the service.

Leader: Light and peace in Jesus Christ.
All: Thanks be to God.

You may wish to provide small candles for participants and light them during the singing of the evening hymn. Signal participants to stand for the hymn.

Evening Hymn (standing)

For sessions one through three, choose from "Christ, Mighty Savior" (*UMH*, no. 684), "O Gladsome Light" (*UMH*, no. 686), or "Now It Is Evening" (*TFWS*, no. 2187); Session Four, "The Day Thou Gavest, Lord, Is Ended" (*UMH*, no. 690); Session Five, "Creator of the Stars of Night" (*UMH*, no. 692) Note: *This ancient tune may be unfamiliar. You may wish to substitute another tune in Long Meter (LM). Tallis Canon may be especially appropriate (UMH, no. 682). See the Metrical Index (UMH, pages 926–27).*

    Ask participants to be seated.

Scripture

    Session One: Matthew 24:36-44
    Session Two: Matthew 3:1-12
    Session Three: Matthew 11:2-11
    Session Four: Matthew 1:18-25
    Session Five: Luke 1:46b-55

Silence (2 minutes. If all participants lit their own candles these may be extinguished during this time. The main candle should remain lit).

Invite participants to stand for the song and prayers.

Song of Praise (The Canticle of Mary or "Tell Out, My Soul" is customary, *UMH*, no. 199 or 200)

Prayers of the People (Spoken: *UMH*, no. 879; Sung: *TFWS*, no. 2201)

The instructor leads the intercessions for the opening session. Course participants will lead in succeeding sessions. If you choose to sing, do so in a "normal," almost "spoken" register. People may remain silent except responses, or they may lift up names of persons or situations related to each petition. Conclude the intercessions with "for the forgiveness of our sins."

Silence (1 minute)

Leader: Hear the good news. If we confess our sins, God is faithful and just and will forgive us our sins and cleanse us from all unrighteousness. In the name of Jesus Christ, we are forgiven.
People: **In the name of Jesus Christ, we are all forgiven.**
All: **Glory to God,** *Amen.*

Lord's Prayer

Blessing

Leader: May the grace of Jesus Christ be with us through the coming night.
People: **Thanks be to God.**

The Peace

NIGHT PRAYER

Light a candle and call everyone to silence (2 minutes).

Leader: Almighty, grant us a peaceful night, free from danger, and peace at our journey's end.
People: **Amen.**

Leader: Let us confess our sins to God—what we have done, what we have left undone, and the promptings of the Holy Spirit we have failed to heed. Let us pray.

Silence (one minute), or sing "Confession" (WS, no. 3138) followed by silence.

Leader: Let us pray.

All: Receive our confession, forgive us, and make us whole.

Leader: In the name of Jesus we are forgiven, cleansed, and healed.

All: In Christ alone we rest. *Amen.*

Song

Choose from "All Praise to Thee, My God, This Night" (*UMH*, no. 682), "Now, on Land and Sea Descending" (*UMH*, no. 685), "God, That Madest Earth and Heaven" (*UMH*, no. 688), "The Day Thou Gavest, Lord, Is Ended" (*UMH*, no. 689), or "Holy Darkness" (*WS*, no. 3141).

Prayers of Commendation

The leader of the first prayer invites everyone to sit and place their palms facing up on their lap, a gesture of release of all things to God. The leader should allow for significant pauses between intercessions. Persons in the class may take turns leading the prayer throughout these commendations.

Prayer leader: Into your hands, O God, into your hands.

People: Into your hands, O God, into your hands.

Prayer leader: The day that has been . . . the people we have seen . . .

People: Into your hands, O God, into your hands.

Prayer leader: The work we have done . . . the work we have left undone . . .

People: Into your hands, O God, into your hands.

Prayer leader: Our families, friends, congregations, and all who work with and care for us . . . Sisters and brothers in Christ throughout the world . . .

People: Into your hands, O God, into your hands.

Prayer leader: All whose work we rarely see . . . All who watch or work or weep while we sleep . . .

People: Into your hands, O God, into your hands.

Prayer leader: The earth and all that sustains it . . . All who have commended themselves to our prayers . . .

People: Into your hands, O God, into your hands.

Prayer leader: Our bodies . . . our breathing . . . the motions of our minds . . . the beating of our hearts . . .

People: Into your hands, O God, into your hands.

Blessing

The Holy One,
Father, Son, Spirit,
Creator, Christ, Advocate,
Mother, Womb, Nurse,
Source, and End of All,
enfold, guide, and bless us
this night and always.

Go in peace.

The Peace

FIVE BASIC PRINCIPLES OF WORSHIP

1. God's word is primary.
2. Active congregational participation is crucial.
3. Spontaneity and order are equally important.
4. Worship should be relevant and inclusive.
5. Worship is communion.

Excerpt from *Worshiping with United Methodists: A Guide for Pastors and Church Leaders* by Hoyt Hickman. Copyright © 2007 Abingdon. Used by permission.

BASIC PATTERN OF WORSHIP

ENTRANCE

The people gather in Christ's name and assemble as Christ's body to begin their worship of God with praise and prayer.

PROCLAMATION AND RESPONSE

The scriptures are read and preached, and the people respond. The responses may include psalms, songs, anthems, hymns, drama, or art. Responses to the sermon may include a call to discipleship, confession of faith, services of the baptismal covenant, and prayers for the church and the world.

THANKSGIVING AND COMMUNION

The people are invited to the Lord's table, confess their sin, receive pardon, embrace one another in the peace of Christ, and offer themselves in praise and thanksgiving, with gifts of bread and wine, for God's mighty acts of salvation. The people receive the broken bread and poured cup as the Body and Blood of Christ, and give thanks for all they have received.

SENDING FORTH

Having praised God, heard God's word, responded, and been fed at the Lord's table, the people are sent out in the world to live as Christ's body, redeemed by his blood, in the power of the Holy Spirit.

OBSERVATIONS AND FEEDBACK FOR WORSHIP PLANNERS

Team Members:
Anchor Image:
Series/Seasonal Theme:
Service Theme:
Local Context:
Space Design:

Energy

Before Entrance: "Energy Challenge!" Attention and energy scattered in multiple directions

Entrance: Synchronizing the Assembly through Whole Body Actions

Word/Response: Active, Attentive Listening

Modes of Energy in Response(s): invitation, confessing faith, prayers, baptism, receiving members, and so on

Table: Confession, Pardon, Peace, Offering, Great Thanksgiving, Distribution, After Receiving

Sending: Active/Propulsion into the World

Presence*

Prayerfulness ("heavy on awe and mystery, light on answers and recipes")

Comfort in Your Own Skin

Confidence

Care with words ("when we do use words, make them really count")

Leadership

Engaging the *worshipers* in worship by embodying the energy and action needed for each movement and moment in worship—Entrance, Word/Response, Table, Sending

Flow

Minor Transitions—between elements within movements

Bearings—between movements

To Entrance:

Entrance to Word/Response:

Word/Response to Table:

Table to Sending:

*Source for categories and quotes: *Strong, Loving and Wise: Presiding in Liturgy* by Robert W. Hovda, (Liturgical Press, 1983), 34–35.

WHAT AFFECTS PERCEPTIONS OF WORSHIP?

[Space
    Ambience
Energy
    Pre]sence
Leadership
    Flow

SLICE
CORE VALUES OF VITAL WORSHIP
IN THE UNITED METHODIST CHURCH

"S"—**Sacramental**: Congregations continue to grow in the richness of their sacramental life in worship and ministry.

"L"—**Liturgical**: Worship is primarily the work of the people, not simply the work of the "folks up front" or the production of the worship planning team.

"I"—**Indigenous**: Worship consistently reflects the best gifts of your particular people gathered in your particular time and place.

"C"—**Connected**: Worship is connected and continues to connect worshipers to Christ, to one another, to all Christians in all times and places, and to ministry that reaches all the world.

"E"—**Embodied**: Worship calls and enables worshipers to offer themselves to God in many ways, including with their bodies.

SACRAMENTAL

How do you celebrate the sacraments as fully as you can (words/gestures/music/"holy hardware"/movement in space) where you are?

How do you help people live out the sacraments and the Great Thanksgiving in daily life?

SERVICES OF THE BAPTISMAL COVENANT

Baptism, Confirmation/Reception of New Members, Reaffirmation

CELEBRATING THE RITUAL

How you say the words/offer the prayers
Gestures
Music (before, during, after the service)
Location/size/prominence of the font/amount and form of water
Movement and orientation of the congregation

LIVING THE RITUAL

What do you do to help people actively in their daily lives?
Renounce the spiritual forces of wickedness?
Repent of their sin?
Resist evil, injustice, and oppression in whatever forms they present themselves?
Embrace and serve Jesus Christ as Savior and Lord?
Live in union with the whole church open to all people?
Serve as Christ's representatives in the world?

Holy Communion

Regular and Special Occasions

Celebrating the Ritual

How you say the words/offer the prayers?
Invitation, Confession and Pardon, Peace, Presentation of Gifts, Great Thanksgiving, Distribution, Post-Communion Prayer, Sending forth
Gestures
Music (before, during, after the service)
Location/size/prominence of the Lord's table
Movement and orientation of the congregation

Living the Ritual

What do you do to help people in their daily lives "be for the world the body of Christ redeemed by his blood?"

> *Preach the good news to the poor.*
> *Proclaim release to the captives and recovery of sight to the blind(ed).*
> *Set at liberty those who are oppressed.*
> *Announce that the time has come when God will save God's people.*
> *Heal the sick, feed the hungry, eat with sinners.*

What do you do to help people in their daily lives offer themselves "in praise and thanksgiving as a holy and living sacrifice in union with Christ's offering for us" (*UMH*, 10)?

LITURGICAL

Liturgy—Greek ➔ leitourgia ➔ laos *(people),* ergon *(work)* ➔ *"work of the people"*

How is worship truly the **work** *of the* **people**—all the people—and not just the "folks up front?"

Exercise: Review Worship Bulletins

At each point in the service ask the following questions:

- Who is leading?
- Who is working (include tech folks)? How?
- Who is becoming more engaged? How?
- Who is becoming less engaged or disengaged entirely? How?

Looking at the service overall, ask the following questions:

- Who is engaged?
- Who is disengaged?
- Given your strengths as a congregation, what might be done with the *flow* or the *actions* of the service to encourage more engagement by more people more of the time?

How does the design of worship in your particular setting help people both expand their repertoire and make worship their own over time (repetition, following a basic pattern allowing for improvement/creativity)?

INDIGENOUS

No "plug-and-play!" No "one right way!"

How is your worship truly the *work of* **these particular people** *in your* **particular community** *at this* **particular** *time?*

These Particular People

Describe a time when your worship seemed to express the voice, cadences, and movement of these particular people best? What factors contributed to make the worship "click?"

What gifts could the people *in your congregation* have that can be offered in worship?

- Music
- Arts
- Performance
- Technology
- Design
- Cultural heritage/Tradition
- Expert perspective (training, skill, and life experience/testimony)

What process do you or your congregation have in place to *find*, *evaluate*, and *deploy* the gifts of the people in your congregation?

Your Particular Community

If the congregation is the *public* face of the Christian faith, your worship must take seriously the various *publics* with which you and the people within your congregation have relationships:

- those persons within the immediate neighborhood/region of your public worship space
- those persons in the social networks of your existing congregation

- work connections
- nearby family connections
- home neighborhood connections
- school connections
- leisure/sports place connections
- shopping place connections
- "virtual" connections within reasonable driving distance of the worship space
- community service connections (clubs, organizations, and the like)

What gifts might these different categories of people have to offer your worship?

What process do you or your congregation have in place to invite and include these people in your worship?

This Particular Time

What planning processes or actions help your congregation locate worship in the here and now instead of some golden past or wished for future?

- Prayer requests and prayers reflecting current concerns and realities
- Music with texts or tunes that capture lived realities
- Preaching
- Sacraments
- Actions in worship that keep people engaged
- Appropriate use of technology

CONNECTED

Worship is religion, a kind of relinking, enacted in public ritual. Christian worship specifically relinks those gathered to God, to one another, to the wider world, and to all Christians in all times and places.

During Holy Communion we pray for the Spirit to make us "one with Christ, one with each other, and one in ministry to all the world."

Exercise: Bulletin Review

One with Christ in our triune God

Mark places in your bulletin where your worship *expresses*, *affirms*, or *enacts* unity with Christ and the Trinity.

- Expresses: says it (hymns, sermons)
- Affirms: agrees with it (creeds, calls to worship)
- Enacts: makes it happen (sacraments)

One with One Another

Mark places in your bulletin where your worship *expresses*, *affirms*, or *enacts* unity with one another.

- Here and now
- With people around the world and across time
- In ways that witness to how God's "future" salvation happening now

One way we share our connection with one another is through a common pattern of worship. What pattern(s) of worship do you see at work in your worship?

United Methodist Basic Pattern/Ecumenical/Ancient Ordo

Entrance, Word/Response, Thanksgiving/Communion, Sending

Aim: The people of God encounter God, offer themselves, and are sent out into the world in ministry

Revival/Seeker Basic Pattern

Praise/Preliminaries, Preaching for a Decision, Invitation

Aim: To lead sinners/seekers to an encounter with/decision for Jesus Christ

Specific Cultural Pattern

Forms and aims vary by culture.

Sunday School/Creative Worship Pattern

Announcements of Programs/Presentations/Emphases, Praising God (variety/novelty), Special Music (creative, unusual), Teaching (children through special lessons or programs, adults through sermons), Closing Song or Action (if not repeated then summarizing what was learned/focused on that day)

Aim: To teach/encounter God creatively

American Protestant Aesthetic "Preaching Service" Pattern

Praise, Confessions (faith and/or sin), Offering, "Oratorical" Pastoral Prayer, Choral Music (usually by robed choirs, "high" art and poetry, classical music/hymns), Preaching, Benediction

Aim: To inspire the spirits of the worshipers

With what does this pattern or mix of patterns help connect you? In what ways does your pattern or mix of patterns create distractions or disconnections?

One in Ministry to all the World

Invite participants to move their hands as you describe each of these ways worship connects us to the world.

Hands up: Intercession for the church and the world

How does prayer in worship help worshipers offer the entire church and the whole world to God in prayer?

Hands on: Ministry in the world

Where in your worship do you help people connect with group or personal ministries of mercy, reconciliation, and justice (examples: passing of the peace, announcements, stories of/by community ministries or missions, prayers, inviting people to services, and so on)?

Hands out: Projections of money or influence flowing from worship

How are resources collected in worship specifically identified and channeled for ministries in and beyond your congregation or community (offering, Communion offering, special offerings, and the like)?

Overall: How do the patterns that emerge from your worship services reflect

- the presence and balance of elements of connectedness
- areas where connection occurs well (strengths)
- opportunities to expand these strengths into other areas of ministry

EMBODIED

We love God and worship God with our whole selves—mind, body, and spirit. And our selves are not simply our own, but are always inherited, received, and shared.

Worship that enables us to offer ourselves to God makes the best use of our whole selves as embodied community at each moment of the worship service.

Key terms

Flow

Alignment of Actions/Words

Where are your current strengths in each of these areas? Where can you leverage existing strengths to grow more strengths?

Focus Areas for Embodied Worship

The use, design, and redesign(ability) of the worship space. Examples:

- Room for movement
- An inviting table
- A visible and often used font
- Space that belongs to the worshiping community

The Voicing of Scripture

Sung, spoken, chanted, dramatized, art, music, drums, dance, rhythm

The Lifting Up of Praise and Prayer

Voice, volume, gesture, posture, poetry, song, embodied prayer

Enacting the sermon and sacraments

Sermon as enactment not of manuscript but of "Word of God" alive and active in your midst

Presiding over the sacraments—*how* the ritual is enacted by presider and people and *how* we all interact with the basic elements of water, Spirit, voice, Body, Blood, bath, Word, and meal

Alignment of Actions, Space, and Words (Use a bulletin from one or more worship services to review.)

1. Where in our worship are the actions and positions of our bodies generally best aligned with the words we are saying (Leadership, Presence, Energy)?
2. Where in our worship do changes in movement or position seem to be most helpful in the transition from completed action to new action (Flow, Bearings)?
3. What elements in our worship space seem best aligned with our actions? What adjustments to the worship space might we make to better accomplish our goals (Space Design)?
4. What can we learn, add, or change to address areas where actions, changes in actions, or the worship space seem to impede or be irrelevant to what we are doing?

ADDITIONAL RESOURCES

ONLINE

United Methodist Worship website: http://www.umcworship.org

This website is a comprehensive and constantly expanding collection of resources for worship planning, church music, and preaching, including thousands of articles, tips, and downloadable music (scores and mp3).

United Methodist Worship blog: http://umcworship.blogspot.com

Worship-related Facebook groups: UMC Worship, UMC Music, UMC Preachers, Worship& Song

PRINT

By Water and the Spirit: Making Connections for Identity and Ministry by Gayle Carlton Felton (Discipleship Resources, 1997). This title is a study guide to assist people in understanding The United Methodist Church's theology and practice of baptism. It includes the full text of the teaching document on baptism reaffirmed by the 2012 General Conference.

Come to the Waters: Baptism and Our Ministry of Welcoming Seekers and Making Disciples by Daniel T. Benedict Jr. (Discipleship Resources, 1996). *Come to the Waters* looks at the growing number of seekers, particularly those with little or no Christian background, and proposes a contemporary update of an early Christian method of leading seekers to full Christian commitment.

Extending the Table: A Guide for a Ministry of Home Communion Serving by Mark W. Stamm (Discipleship Resources, 2009). This is a comprehensive guide for congregations that provide Holy Communion to persons unable to attend worship.

The New Handbook of the Christian Year Based on the Revised Common Lectionary by Hoyt L. Hickman, Don E. Saliers, Laurence Hull Stookey, and James F. White (Abingdon, 1992) is a comprehensive resource for understanding and observing the Christian year.

Living into the Mystery: A United Methodist Guide for Celebrating Holy Communion, edited by Taylor Burton-Edwards (Discipleship Resources, 2007) is a collection of essays by leading worship scholars designed to help congregations and pastors celebrate the sacrament richly within their context. It includes a study guide for small-group learning.

The United Methodist Book of Worship: Pastor's Pocket Edition (The United Methodist Publishing House, 1994). This resource contains excerpts from the *Book of Worship* needed for ministering to people outside their usual worship space. Available from Cokesbury.

The United Methodist Worship Planning Calendar (The United Methodist Publishing House, published annually).

This Holy Mystery: A United Methodist Understanding of Holy Communion by Gayle Carlton Felton (Discipleship Resources, 2004). This is a study guide to assist understanding of The United Methodist Church's theology and practice of Holy Communion. It includes the full text of the document on Holy Communion reaffirmed by the 2012 General Conference.

CPSIA information can be obtained
at www.ICGtesting.com
Printed in the USA
LVHW011112060819
626629LV00002B/3/P